HOW TO
WRITE BETTER
IN ONE HOUR

HOW TO
WRITE BETTER
IN ONE HOUR

George Mair

Illustrated by Paul Harrington

A SCARBOROUGH BOOK
STEIN AND DAY/*Publishers*/New York

FIRST SCARBOROUGH BOOKS EDITION 1983
Copyright © 1983 by George Mair
All rights reserved, Stein and Day, Incorporated
Designed by Louis A. Ditizio
Printed in the United States of America
STEIN AND DAY/*Publishers*
Scarborough House
Briarcliff Manor, N.Y. 10510

Library of Congress Cataloging in Publication Data

Mair, George.
  How to write better in one hour.

  1. English language—Rhetoric—Self-instruction.
I. Title.
PE1409.5.M34   1983   808'.042   83-42971
ISBN 0-8128-6206-6 (pbk.)

CONTENTS

YES, IT IS TRUE . . .

. . . You Can Be a Better Writer in One Hour

Spend one hour reading and working in this book and you'll be a better writer. That one hour will:

- Help you influence other people
- Promote your own success
- Give power to your ideas

In the One Hour You Spend With This Book, You Will:

- Learn the basic *Communication Process*
- Find out what distorts clear communication
- Discover the three myths of communication
- Be able to write strong, clean sentences and paragraphs
- Eliminate trite and awkward words from your writing
- Learn the style and tone of professional writers
- Find out the *Ten Basic Secrets of Power Writing*®

NO, you will not become an instant Ernest Hemingway, James Michener, or William Shakespeare. And you will not be a better writer at all if you don't do the work in the book. But if you spend one hour reading and writing as you are told to do in this book, IT WILL WORK. YOU WILL BE A BETTER WRITER.

This learning system has been tested on several thousand people. It has worked for them. It can work for you. The Chief Executive Officer of a major steel company* who took this Power Writing Program at the University of Chicago says:

> I believe that the Power Writing Program has helped my writing skills. I think the most important contribution is the ability to communicate ideas more concisely and clearly.

"The Ability to Communicate Ideas More Concisely and Clearly."

That's what this book can help you improve in just one hour.

The owner of a major midwestern corporation* says:

> Yes, the program is teaching me to write better. . . . Your program was most dynamic, very

---

*Names furnished by author on request.

stimulating, and extremely beneficial. I would recommend it to anyone who spends his time in communication with others because, most important, it will improve one's thought process.

REMEMBER! This program will not work unless you do. You must do all the work called for in this book, or it will not work for you as it has for thousands of others.

ENOUGH.

LET'S START.

TURN THE PAGE.

FIRST, in the space below, write three sentences describing something you know very well. It could be a place, a process, a person, an experience you have had, something you have seen or heard or felt—anything.

DO IT NOW. Write a three-sentence paragraph about something you know well.

START. *I know a great deal.*

1. About reading. The one way

things for my get thing is for you

work you a lot of reading.

2. I always enjoy listening too dancing to music.

STOP. *3. my children get older*

We'll get back to these three sentences later.

to write

WHY PEOPLE WRITE

Most people don't like to write. It is painful for them, and it lets other people peek into the writer's brain. Even professional writers hate to write and think up excuses to avoid it.

Writing is painful because, too often, we write only for *negative* reasons:

- FEAR—You may write because you are afraid of what might happen if you don't write. You may write to protect your rear end from unpleasant things happening.
- GUILT—You may write from guilt. You write a friend or relative because you are embarrassed at having neglected them for so long.
- PRESSURE—You may be pressured to write something by a boss, the government, or someone with power over you.

All of these reasons are *negative.* No wonder you hate to write!

Instead, try writing for *positive* reasons:

- INFLUENCE—Expand your influence among friends, family, and colleagues by writing. Spread your ideas and enlarge the circle of people touched by your thoughts.

- BUILD SUCCESS—Make writing work for you. It can convince others of your abilities. It can inspire admiration. It can help your career advancement. It can enhance your personal life.

In short, learn to write effectively and for positive reasons for your own personal success.

The Five Steps in Getting an Idea Across

There are five steps in getting an idea across to another person. This is the basic *Communications Process*.

1. IDEA INTO YOUR BRAIN—It starts as an idea in your brain that you want to get into my brain.

2. TRANSLATE IN CODE—You have to translate the idea in your brain into a code that can be sent to me. The code may be squiggly lines on a piece of paper (writing); body language (gestures); or sound vibrations (talking).

3. PASSING THE CODED MESSAGE—Next you have to pass the coded idea to me. Maybe you mail it in a letter or direct it to my ears by speaking.

4. DECODING THE IDEA MESSAGE—Now that I have gotten your coded idea message, I have to decode it in my brain.

5. IDEA IN MY BRAIN—Now what was an idea in your brain has become an idea in my brain.

That's the *Communication Process*. If everything

works perfectly, it will end up with exactly the same idea in my brain as you have in your brain.

Unfortunately, that rarely happens.

STOP.

THE five steps of the Communication Process are listed below. Write a number by each one giving the order in which they happen.

DO IT NOW.

Translate Idea Message into Code
Idea in Sender's Brain
Idea in Receiver's Brain
Pass Idea Message from Sender to Receiver
Decode the Idea Message

CORRECT ANSWER: From top to bottom, you should have numbered the steps in the Communications Process: 2, 1, 5, 3, 4.

COMMUNICATION FILTERS

Idea messages rarely end up exactly as sent because of three *filters* that distort them. These three filters are:

1. VAGUE AND IMPRECISE MEANING—One word may have more than one meaning. "Lead" has twenty different meanings in the dictionary. "Quarter" has seventeen, and "wave" has nine. If our use of words is unclear, the idea message will be unclear.

2. TROUBLE PASSING MESSAGE—Another troublesome communication filter occurs when we have trouble passing the message. Maybe the sender of the idea message does it in a foreign language. Sometimes the foreign language is *English,* but it is filled with specialized jargon so the average person does not understand it. For example, an engineer might call something:

A solid-state barrier access plane activating system

In plain language, he means a doorknob.

One of the world's great tap-dancers wrote a book

"Neonate" means newborn child in doctor jargon

about this kind of filter. In it, this tap dancer talks about the threat of clarity. He says that language is used by high priests, lawyers, critics, and government employees to *conceal* meaning instead of passing along an idea.

This special jargon not only covers up meaning and keeps outsiders from knowing what's happening, it gives the writer or talker an elite status. This tap dancer, for example, dares any doctor to explain the difference between saying, "a newborn child" and saying, "neonate."

The famous tap dancer is also a former U.S. Senator and one of the leading scholars on language in the country. His name is S. I. Hayakawa.

3. TRIGGER WORDS—We are all captives of our experiences, training, and prejudices. Trigger words provoke an emotional reaction for the receiver of the idea message that colors the way he or she gets the message.

For example, carefully study this list of words:

Nazi
Hubert Humphrey ~~#~~   U S President
Brooke Shields
Jew
John F. Kennedy
Dallas Cowboys
Richard Nixon
Tom Selleck
Cuba
Ralph Nader

STOP.

GO BACK. Put a check mark by every word or phrase to which you had an *emotional* reaction—positive or negative. Then come back here and continue reading.

Did you check at least one word or phrase? Most people do. That means if you received an idea message about that subject, you are preconditioned. You are preset to receive it either negatively or positively, which distorts the idea.

STOP AND WRITE.

In the space below, list the three filters that distort the way people receive idea messages from each other.

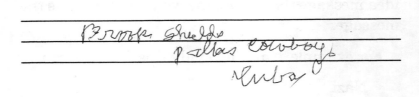

CORRECT ANSWERS: Vague and Imprecise Meaning; Trouble Passing the Message; and Trigger Words.

THREE MYTHS OF COMMUNICATION

The three filters distort the way we receive an idea message. There are also three myths that distort the way the sender sends the message.

We are talking only about people who want to send a *clear* message. As we noted earlier, sometimes people want to *look* as if they are trying to send a message but aren't really. The Secretary of State under Harry S. Truman was Dean Acheson. He said memos are not meant to communicate. They are meant to protect the writer of the memo. We are not talking about that here. We are talking about when the sender wants to communicate.

Here are the three myths that make it hard for the sender to communicate successfully:

1. CAPTIVE AUDIENCE—The first myth is that we have a captive audience, that, because we write something, other people *must* read it and understand it.

Bosses and other people in power suffer from this myth. The truth is that, even when people are *required* by their jobs to read something, it is no guarantee that they will.

The best way to get people to read your writing is to make them *want* to read it.

BIG WORDS = BIG MAN

2. **BIG WORDS = BIG MAN**—The second myth is that big words make a big person. Complicated, long words will impress everyone with how smart you are. This may be a wonderful ego-trip, but it doesn't get ideas across. It doesn't influence people with ideas.

For example, read the next paragraph. Then, on the blank line below it, write a simple translation of what the writer said in that paragraph.

> Upon arrival at the location, personal observations were made of the situation that existed at that point in time, and the decision was made and implemented by this person to proceed with the pacification of the indigenous populace and territory.

_____

Hard isn't it? The writer is trying to impress us with all those big words, but that doesn't give us a clear idea of what he is saying.

The fellow who might have written the paragraph above was the Roman emperor Julius Caesar. He might have written that paragraph, but he didn't. He communicated a similar idea to us by simply saying,

I came. I saw. I conquered.

That is a simple, direct way of communicating his thoughts. That is what we must all try to do: communicate in a simple and direct way.

SAFETY BEFORE CLARITY

3. SAFETY BEFORE CLARITY—The third myth of communication is that protecting your backside is more important than getting an idea across. Lawyers, doctors, politicians, and other professionals load up a poor sentence with every "if" "and," and "but" they can find. They want to protect themselves from making a mistake and don't care about clear writing.

Try this for clear meaning:

Upon receipt by Ajax at its home office, either before the discontinuance of premium payments for an employee's insurance under this part or within twelve months thereafter, of due proof, that the employee, while insured under this part, before attaining the age of sixty years, and before termination of employment with a participant employer, became totally and permanently disabled within the meaning of this section, namely, that, due to sickness or injury, the employee is not engaged in his or any other gainful occupation and will continue to be unable to engage in any gainful occupation for which he is, or may reasonably become, fitted by education, training or experience, and that the employee has been so disabled continuously for at least nine months, then, provided timely written notice of claim for extended insurance has been given and provided, further, that the Ajax Company is allowed the opportunity to examine the person of the employee when and as often as it may reasonably require before approving the proof . . .

HELP! STOP! I CAN'T STAND IT ANYMORE!

In the interests of both our sanity, I stopped. That was the first 167 words of *one sentence* that runs a total of 335 words!

This is the kind of garbage dumped into insurance policies by lawyers. It is not intended to communicate an idea clearly. It is intended to cover the company and the lawyer's rear end.

STOP.

LIST THE THREE MYTHS OF COMMUNICATION BELOW.

_____

_____

_____

CORRECT ANSWERS: Captive Audience; Big Words = Big Man; Safety before Clarity.

A SUPER STAR

A SUPER STAR SYSTEM OF POWER WRITING®

Now we're ready to learn the *ten* steps in *A SUPER STAR* system of power writing. These ten rules of *A SUPER STAR* system of power writing will make you a powerful and convincing writer. They will make people *want* to read what you write.

The name, *A SUPER STAR* system, will help you remember the ten rules. Each letter in the name *A SUPER STAR* stands for one of the ten rules.

Rule 1. **A**UDIENCE

The first rule and the "A" in *A SUPER STAR* system of power writing is *AUDIENCE.*

Before you even start writing, think about who your audience is. Get a mental picture of the one person who is typical of your audience. Write directly to that one person. Gear your style, language, tone, and approach to just that one person.

What is important to that one person? How can you make your idea personally important to that person?

What will capture your audience's attention? It should appeal to something that means a lot to your audience. It might be a financial reward, prestige, power, public admiration, sex appeal, or protection from loss or pain.

Suppose you are writing to your boss asking for a raise. In it's simplest form, you could write, "I want more money for what I do." You are saying what *you* want. Now, change that around to something that the boss wants.

STOP.

TURN THE PAGE.

ON THE LINES BELOW, WRITE A ONE SENTENCE APPEAL TO YOUR BOSS FOR A RAISE. PUT IT IN WORDS THAT MAKE IT APPEALING TO THE BOSS.

_____

_____

Others have done this same exercise. Here are some of the results. Circle the one that you think would be most appealing to your boss—the audience for this letter:

A. I have worked hard, been loyal, and deserve more money.
B. I have a new baby and need more money.
C. A fair raise is cheaper than hiring/training someone new.
D. I am a simply wonderful and deserving person.

The approach in C is probably the best one. It is the only one that is pitched toward what could be important to the *audience*. It is focused on avoiding trouble and expense for the boss.

Rule 2. SHORT AND SIMPLE

Write short. Write simply. Make it easy to read quickly. Avoid long, complicated sentences.

As a guide, test your writing with the 3-20-7 yardstick.

No word longer than 3 syllables.
No sentence longer than 20 words.
No paragraph longer than 7 sentences.

Obviously, you will want to add variety to your writing by having words and paragraphs of varying length. And there may be a special word longer than three syllables that fits perfectly in what you are trying to say. However, the problem in today's writing is not people writing too short but people writing too long.

So apply the 3-20-7 rule as often as you can. Challenge every word, sentence, or paragraph that violates that rule.

David Belasco, the great American theatrical producer, once said: "If you can't write your idea on the back of my calling card, you don't have a clear idea."

That is a good test.

Next time you get ready to pass along an idea, try writing it out on the back of a calling card. If it doesn't fit, maybe you should rethink it.

In fact, since it is such a good test, let's try it right now.

At the beginning of this book, you wrote a short paragraph about something you know well. Remember? Without going back, tell me what the basic idea in that paragraph is.

STOP.

TURN THE PAGE.

PORTABLE TOOTHED
OSCILLATING
HAIR ALIGNER

KEEP IT SIMPLE

WRITE THE BASIC IDEA OF YOUR OPENING PARA-
GRAPH IN THE SPACE BELOW. THIS IS EXACTLY
THE SIZE OF A CALLING CARD. WRITE LARGE
ENOUGH FOR THE AVERAGE PERSON TO READ IT.

STOP.

CIRCLE THE QUOTATION BELOW THAT MOST CLOSELY MEETS OUR 3-20-7 TEST.

A. "After weeks of tough talk, apparent inconsistency, and alarms about a revival of the cold war, the Administration last week seemed to have got its foreign policy act together."

B. "We meet in an hour of grief and challenge. Dag Hammerskjold is dead."

C. "Learned scholars in learned books on mass psychology have come to the conclusion that it is only due to the chance absence of the right kind of demagogic mass leader that we do not go on all fours or are not all nudists, since the masses 'probably' fall easy prey to any superior salesman, whatever his goods."

B is obviously the only one to meet the test. It is the opening line in President John F. Kennedy's September 25, 1961, speech to the United Nations. It is not only short and simple. It was a strong opening in terms of his *audience* and its emotional state at the time.

The other two are neither short nor simple. A is the opening line of the lead story in *Time* Magazine, July 3, 1978. It is a long, awkward, and complicated sentence for a supposedly popular audience.

C is a quotation from Professor Peter Drucker, known as the man who invented corporate society. Clearly he's not the man who invented short and simple writing.

Use Hook Opening And Close

Rule 3. USE A HOOK

You must capture your reader's attention right away. This is Rule #3 in *A SUPER STAR* system of power writing.

Use a hook to get your reader's attention at the very start of your writing. Get him interested in what you have to say.

Appeal to things that motivate the *reader*—not things that motivate *you*.

Most readers are interested in increasing one or more of the FOUR Ps: PROFIT, PLEASURE, POWER, OR PRESTIGE. Appeal to those interests in your reader.

Don't make the reader wander through a jungle of words. Make him decide he *wants* to read what you are saying right away. If you don't, he may give up before you've made your point.

STOP.

CIRCLE ONE OR MORE OF THE FOLLOWING OPEN-INGS IF THEY MAKE YOU WANT TO FIND OUT WHAT COMES NEXT AFTER THE OPENING LINES.

    A. The romance seemed sweetly improbable from the night it began.

    B. In the connection of the church and state, I have considered the former as subservient only, and relative, to the latter; a salutary maxim, if in fact as well as in narrative it had ever been held sacred.

C. Before every game, Ron Luciano removes a pint bottle from his footlocker and takes a long swig.

D. On any given day, the management of Ralph's Grocery Company knows precisely how well a brand of canned peaches or facial tissue or razor blades is selling and why.

E. Charity Sweetness sits in the toilet eating her two hard-boiled eggs while I'm having my ham sandwich and coffee in the kitchen.

F. There was a woman who was beautiful, who started with all the advantages, yet she had no luck.

G. As we all know, only one shift is available for commercial work, which gives us a production capacity of 33 tons of strand per week.

H. Business success lies in following eight simple rules.

Which ones did you pick?

Obviously, the openings you picked will tell you something about yourself as a reader and what is important to you. The point of this exercise is that, for the opening lines above, *you were the audience* (Rule #1). No two people are the same audience. The point is that, if you know your audience, you can write an opening hook for that particular audience.

The opening line examples were from these sources:

A. A story in *People* magazine on the marriage of Princess Caroline and Philippe Junot (since gone on the rocks). It would catch the attention of sentimental romantics.

B. Volume Three of *The Decline and Fall of the Roman Empire* by Edward Gibbons. Few people would be hooked by this poorly written sentence.

C. A sports story on baseball umpire Ron Luciano. It might hook sports fans.

D. A *New York Times* story on computerized inventory. It might attract the attention of retailers and business types.

E. The opening from a book by Bernard Malamud. Most people get hooked on this one.

F. The opening line from a D. H. Lawrence story. Most women get hooked on this one.

G. From an internal memo at Inland Steel Corporation. It does not have much appeal even to those concerned with the subject. For example, it opens with, "As you all know..." If that is true, why say it?

H. The opening line from a *USA Today* news story. It is a good hook for anyone interested in business.

STOP.

ON THE BLANK LINES BELOW, WRITE AN OPENING HOOK FOR A
LETTER, MEMO, OR STORY ON ANY SUBJECT THAT YOU KNOW
WELL.

_____

_____

Later on, show this opening to a friend or col-
league and ask whether he or she wants to hear the
rest of what you have to say on the subject. If not,
you haven't appealed to one of the FOUR Ps that
interest that person.

Rule 4. PURGE POMPOSITY

Take the stuffy, puffy, arrogant phrases out of your writing. Challenge every adjective and every adverb. Cut adjectives and adverbs to the bone.

Pompous words are the sign of egomaniacs trying to show off their vocabulary, education, or power.

Here are some examples:

A. Some inventive interpretation of the malleable wordings of the flexible definition of the crime of obscenity.

B. Some internalized values apply generally, but may vary individually, and in these instances the matter of social support blurs a bit.

C. A Zen-schooled, '60s-bred original . . . a measure of his protean gifts . . . his much-bruited Flake Quotient . . . long before his pas de deux with Ronstadt in Africa . . . his quiescent bad-for-business reputation . . . America's first authentically existentialist national politician.

The first is a quote from a bestselling book about sex, and it tells us what? The author is trying to impress us, but it reads as if it had been translated from Japanese and badly at that.

Purge Pomposity

The second is from a book on writing. This may pinpoint one of the main problems about writing in this country. The people who teach writing are lousy writers themselves.

Finally, the third selection is from a *Newsweek* magazine story on former governor Jerry Brown of California. This was the lead story, and *Newsweek* is supposedly a popular news journal written for the average person on the street. I suspect this incomprehensible piece is written by the writer for other writers. It seems to me this is designed to impress colleagues and not to get an idea across to the reader.

Here is a re-creation of an exchange of letters between a New York City plumber and the U.S. Bureau of Standards in Washington, D.C. We have edited them down for convenience:

Dear U.S. Bureau of Standards,
I am a New York City plumber and find hydrochloric acid fine for cleaning drains, but I want to know if it is okay to use it.

Dear New York Plumber,
The efficacy of hydrochloric acid is indisputable, but the chlorine residue is incompatible with metallic permanence.

Dear Bureau of Standards,
I am glad you agree with me. Thanks for the help.

Dear New York Plumber,

We cannot assume responsibility for the production of toxic and noxious residues with hydrochloric acid and suggest you adopt an alternate procedure.

Dear Bureau of Standards,

Thanks for backing me up. The hydrochloric acid works like a dream.

Dear New York Plumber,

Don't use hydrochloric acid—it eats the hell out of pipes!

There are many other examples of pomposity in the mindless phrases that people sprinkle throughout their letters and memos. Here are some common ones:

Instead of	*Use This*
absolutely complete	complete
advance planning	planning
ask the question	ask
assembled together	assembled
continue on	continue
enclosed herewith	enclosed
each and every	each or every—not both
exactly identical	identical
expired and terminated	expired or terminated—not both
repeat again	repeat
the reason is because	because
in regard to	about
on the part of	for

with reference to	about
in view of	because
in the event of	if
on behalf of	for
for the purpose of	for
in the majority of instances	usually
as of this date	today
at the present time	now
in a position to	can, may

The left hand column contains only a few examples of the many pompous, unclear words and phrases that should be stripped out of your writing.

STOP.

EDIT OR REWRITE THE FOLLOWING EXAMPLES OF POMPOUS WRITING. EVERY UNNECESSARY WORD, PHRASE, AND POMPOSITY SHOULD BE TAKEN OUT. YOU CAN TAKE WORDS AWAY, ADD WORDS, MOVE WORDS, SAY THE SAME THING IN A DIFFERENT WAY. GO TO IT.

A. We would like to take this opportunity to congratulate you on the occasion of your advancement in the company.

YOUR EDITED REWRITE:

_____

_____

B. At the present time, we find it beyond our capability.

YOUR EDITED REWRITE:

_____

_____

C. Please initiate a thorough investigation into the circumstances surrounding the occurrence.

YOUR EDITED REWRITE:

_____

_____

D. Disclosure of the requested information is voluntary and there are no adverse effects against you for not disclosing such information; however, failure to provide information will result in the employee not being enrolled in the course.

YOUR EDITED REWRITE:

_____

_____

E. When a metallic receptacle containing common liquids is subjected to careful and continuous scrutiny of a deliberate nature, the liquid which it is the nature and purpose of said receptacle to contain will not, in point of fact, undergo a phase change entering into a gaseous form at any point in time within the duration of the aforementioned scrutiny.

_____

_____

Here are my suggested solutions for purging the pomposity from the five examples. Your solution may be different and still be good. The objective is to make it easier to understand the idea being transmitted by the writing. If your solution does that, it is as right as my suggested ones below.

Yes, I know they are upside down. That's to save you from yourself and temptation before you complete the exercise.

A. Congratulations on your promotion.
B. We can't do it now.
C. Find out what happened.
D. If you don't answer the questions, you don't get into the course.
E. A watched pot never boils.

Rule 5. EVERYDAY LANGUAGE

Use everyday language. Write as people talk, and do not use jargon, technical words, and foreign phrases. Most people don't understand them, and they interfere with passing your message clearly.

Test your writing by letting someone who doesn't know your professional jargon read it. See if they understand the message you are trying to send.

A Federal Aviation Administration report on the crash of an American Airlines airplane into a mountain in Virginia said the accident was caused by:

"Excessive terrain closure rate"

In other words, it flew into the ground.

A sign at the Monterey School of Languages warns,

"Luminaries should be de-energized during periods of maximum outside brightness."

In other words, when the sun is out, turn off the lights.

A point that few people realize about writing is that the reader *hears* what he or she is reading. That's why I say you should write as people talk— simply and naturally.

Avoid using adjectives as nouns, nouns as adjectives, or nouns as verbs. "Good" examples of bad language include:

A. It is time to target our goals.
B. The train will platform in Hartford.
C. Detroit is downsizing its cars.
D. The group will prioritize its objectives.
E. The company is on a disincentivization program.
F. The building will be reconfigured.

When using words, think how they *sound* to the reader. Make it easy and pleasant for the reader to *hear* what you have written.

Avoid long words with Latin origins and go for short Anglo-Saxon words. One of Abraham Lincoln's most notable speeches was his Second Inaugural Address. The entire speech runs 701 words. Of the 701 words, 627 are words of *one* or *two syllables.*

STOP.

GO BACK TO THE GOOD EXAMPLES OF BAD LAN-GUAGE THAT ARE LISTED ABOVE. BELOW, RE-WRITE THEM USING *EVERYDAY LANGUAGE*.

A. _____

B. _____

C. _____

D. _____

E. _____

F. _____

Following are my suggested solutions. Upside down again, of course.

A. We should decide on our goals now.
B. The train will stop in Hartford.
C. Detroit is making smaller cars.
D. They will list their objectives in the order of importance.
E. The company is trying to discourage that.
F. We will redesign the building.

Rule 6. RECAP YOUR MATERIAL

Recap or summarize the main points of what you are saying. Let the reader get the main thrust quickly without wading through the entire memo, letter, or report. For example, many top business executives require that all reports have an *executive summary*. This is often at the beginning of the report and not more than one page long.

Newspapers and magazines do the same thing to make it easy for their readers. Newspapers and magazines use sub-headings and boldface summaries in the middle of a page of material. This last technique is called using "windows." An example of a window follows.

TURN THE PAGE.

difficult as the next guy's, and I was expected to handle all kinds of interviews, even of older men and M.B.A.s. I had to be extremely professional and know exactly what I was doing. Still, some people held my age and the fact that I was a woman against me. I was 24 at the time, and I remember one 30-year-old Vietnam veteran who refused to be interviewed by me."

> "I did so much traveling, I'd just have time to dump out one suitcase of dirty clothes and repack with clean ones."

Despite such occasional problems, Susan persevered, and in October of 1972 was made director of the bank's recruiting staff, a position she held for two years.

"I did so much traveling when I was a recruiter that I was hardly ever home. I'd just have time to dump out one suitcase of dirty clothes and repack with clean ones. I remember times when I wasn't able to catch a plane and ended up taking a train or driving all night to get to my next morning's appointment. But it was a really good experience. I certainly

In letters, you can recap the main point by using a secret. It is a secret that direct mail advertising experts have known for years. It is called, *The Power of the P.S.*

The most eye-catching line in a letter is usually the first line. The second most eye-catching line is the P.S. Use the P.S. for a powerful reinforcement of your main point. Don't waste the power of the P.S. on anything trivial. Use it to recap and reinforce your main point.

Stimulate Reader's Interest

Rule 7. STIMULATE THE READER'S INTEREST

If you used the hook opening we talked about earlier, you have captured the reader's attention at the start.

Now you have to keep it.

Do that by writing in a *personal way*. Write about people—not faceless officials and organizations. Use narration—tell a story. Use anecdotes to illustrate your points. Make your writing come alive by talking about people—their hopes and their fears. The *Wall Street Journal* uses this technique with great success.

For example, an article about Chrysler Corporation trying to get a huge federal government subsidy began with a story about a married couple in Detroit.

It went somewhat like this:

> Gail and John Huddleson want another baby, but Uncle Sam may not let them.
>
> John, a laid-off Chrysler worker, met Gail when she was a cheerleader at St. Emmanual High School, and they got married four years ago. It was a good marriage, and after two years they had little Mary Francis, the first of what Gail prays will be four or five children.
>
> But times have changed, and John has been

out of work for seven months. The young couple are two payments behind in their mortgage. Plans for any more babies are on hold until Uncle Sam decides whether he will bail out Chrysler and give John back his job.

The idea is that you have to draw the reader into your writing. You have to make him *want* to continue reading by talking about people and the real world—not some obscure abstraction.

Appealing to the physical senses of the reader is important. Give him or her concrete examples that can be seen, heard, tasted, smelled, and touched instead of vague or intellectual abstractions.

In this same connection, let's say a word about *endings*.

After you have hooked your reader at the beginning and stimulated him to read to the end, *give him a reward*. Give him or her a good ending, one that leaves him amused, thoughtful, or surprised. In fact, surprise is one of the most pleasant endings you can give him. In short, provide an ending that leaves the reader glad he made the trip with you.

Here is an example of an article about the nuclear accident at Three Mile Island. Note that it incorporates all the elements we have talked about for good writing.

The hook.

Nobody died at Three-Mile Island. The ultimate disaster was avoided—*barely*.

Stimulating the reader by building seriousness and talking about people and the real world.

For that we have luck to thank, not sound engineering and not good judgment. Thousands might have died. They would not have died quickly as by a bullet nor quietly as in their sleep.

Descriptive detail, using a disaster from the past that most readers have heard about.

They would have endured a painful, lingering death from radiation sickness like victims of the Black Death in the Middle Ages.

A fact or new way of looking at something that arouses interest and keeps reader stimulated.

Of all the forms of energy mankind uses, nuclear fisson is the only one we can't turn off or douse at will.

Uses familiar examples that are part of the reader's life and make it easy for reader to identify with the story.

For the average reader, electron volts is hard to understand. So, comparison is drawn with T.N.T., which is somewhat easier to grasp.

A personal picture of a man touched by the disaster, made better because he is a congressman.

You can put out the flame in your living room fireplace and turn off the energy in your car engine with a key.

However, when you make a single uranium atom fission, it immediately releases 180 million electron volts of energy. A pound of uranium has the energy of 8,000 tons of T.N.T.

Miles to the south of Three-Mile Island on that cold March morning of the accident, a pajama-clad congressman, Phil Burton, sat in the den of his federal style townhouse in northwest Washington, D.C. absorbing every television news report that came in.

Surprise ending. The reader's reward. Also, added personal drama involving a living person and not an abstract concept.

Three-Mile Island had been part of the farm of his wife's parents before it became a nuclear plant, and she was visiting them now.

Tell Your Story Right Away

Rule 8. TELL STORY IMMEDIATELY

Tell the reader what you want to say right out front. Cover your main points right away.

Write in the *Pyramid Style*. Start with the most important point at the top of the page and broaden out details as you move down. This is the reverse of how much writing is done. Too often the main point, conclusion, or recommendation is buried pages and pages into the writing. The reader's eyes have usually glazed over by that time, and your main point never penetrates his addled brain.

Malcolm Forbes, President and Editor-in-Chief of *Forbes* Magazine, says this about writing good business letters:

> *Tell what your letter is about in the first paragraph.* One or two sentences. Don't keep your reader guessing or he might file your letter away—even before he finishes it.
>
> In the round file.
>
> People who read business letters are as human as thee and me. Reading a letter shouldn't be a chore—*reward* the reader for the time he gives you."*

---

*Quoted by permission.

Rule 9. ACTIVE AND ALIVE WRITING

Use direct and concrete words. Use the *active voice*. Write in a positive, definite way. Don't be passive, defensive, and cowering. Avoid squishy, higgledy-piggledy, weasel words.

One of the problems with telling people to write in the *active voice* is that most people don't know what that means. It means this: Whoever or whatever is doing the *action* in the sentence should be the *subject* of the sentence.

We all know about George Washington supposedly being involved in chopping down a cherry tree. If we were going to tell that story in one sentence, who will be doing the *action*? Obviously, George will be doing the *action*. Therefore, if we write in the *active voice*, we make George the *subject* of the sentence.

ACTIVE VOICE

George Washington chopped down the cherry tree.

PASSIVE VOICE

The cherry tree was chopped down by George Washington.

STOP.

MARK THE FOLLOWING AS EITHER *PASSIVE* OR *ACTIVE* VOICE.

____ A. The house in McLean was painted by Charles Daro.

____ B. Malcolm fired his money manager last Tuesday.

____ C. It wasn't long before the course was changed by Henry.

____ D. Project Delta was a success.

The second and last of the above were in the active voice. The others were in the passive voice.

STOP.

REWRITE THE SENTENCES BELOW IN THE ACTIVE VOICE.

A. The report was written by Jim Henderson.

_____

B. Your claim is being processed by the accounting department.

_____

C. There has been an increase in sales during 1983.

_____

D. A hearing on Social Security was held by the committee.

_____

Rule 10. REST AND REWRITE

After you have finished writing something, set it aside and do something else for a while. Come back to what you have written a few hours or a day later. REVIEW. REREAD. REWRITE.

The essence of really good writing is REWRITING.

Check to see whether you have applied the other nine rules of *A SUPER STAR* system of power writing.

1. AUDIENCE. Is it geared to the interests of your audience?
2. SHORT AND SIMPLE. The 3-20-7 rule.
3. USE HOOK. Did you capture the reader immediately?
4. PURGE POMPOSITY. Cut out puffy and unnecessary words.
5. EVERYDAY LANGUAGE. Write as people talk—no jargon.
6. RECAP. Summarize main points. Use the power of the P.S.
7. STIMULATE. Hold reader interest. Use a surprise closing.
8. TELL STORY. Pyramid style. Main point, then details.

9. **ACTIVE AND ALIVE.** Direct, concrete words. Active voice.
10. **REST AND REWRITE.** Review. Reread. Rewrite.

The rest and rewrite phase of writing is one of the most important for the creative process to work.

Before beginning to write, have a clear idea of what the final objective is—what idea you are trying to get across.

THE SENTENCE AND THE PARAGRAPH

The Basic Building Blocks of Writing

The sentence and the paragraph are the basic building blocks of good writing. We will talk about them in a moment but first there is something else. It is called *thinking*.

Think before you write, not during. Think what you are trying to say. Decide what is the idea you are trying to get across to other people. Only when you have thought out what you want to say, should you begin writing sentences and paragraphs.

The Sentence

A good sentence consists of a single, clear unit of thought. It is not cluttered.

William Zinsser, one of the best editors in America, says:

> Clutter is the disease of American writing. We are a society strangling in unnecessary words, circular constructions, pompous frills, and meaningless jargon. The secret of good writing

is to strip every sentence to its cleanest components. Simplify, simplify, simplify. Thoreau said it.*

Following are examples of simple, clean sentences, sentences with one thought, clearly stated.

- The store in which the Justice of Peace's court sat smelled of cheese.

- Sell 4,000 shares of Consolidated tomorrow.

- The declarative sentence may be an endangered species.

Here is an example of a sentence that isn't clean or clear.

- The recovery of Constantinople was celebrated as the era of a new empire; the conqueror, alone, and by the right of the sword, renewed his coronation in the church of St. Sophia; and, the name and honours of John Lascaris, his pupil and lawful sovereign, were insensibly abolished.

*Quoted by permission.

A clean and lean sentence has two essential parts: a subject and a predicate (which some people call the verb).

The *subject* is who or what the sentence is about. The *predicate* tells us about the subject. It tells us what the subject does, did, will do, or ought to do.

Good Sentences and Good Paragraphs Don't Have More

The Paragraph

A good paragraph is several sentences grouped together but *still focused on one idea*. Each sentence in the paragraph relates to every other sentence and dwells on the central thought in the paragraph.

The central thought of the paragraph is stated in what is called the *topic sentence*. Traditionally, the *topic sentence* is the first one in the paragraph.

The other sentences in the paragraph expand, explain, or defend the idea stated in the topic sentence. There are several ways these other sentences can do that.

They can:

- **DEFINE.** They can define the idea further.

One way to build a paragraph is using descriptions.

- **DETAIL.** The other sentences can fill out specific details.

- **COMPARE.** They can compare or contrast with other ideas.

Examples

- **EXAMPLE.** They can give examples.

- **ANALYZE.** They may analyze the topic idea.

- **ENDORSEMENTS.** They might cite endorsements for the topic idea.

These are just some of the ways that the supporting sentences can expand, explain, or defend the central idea of the topic sentence.

A good paragraph has unity, consistency and order

THREE PRINCIPLES OF GOOD PARAGRAPHS

The well-written paragraph has three basic traits. While there is some overlap among the three, each is distinctive enough to deserve separate attention.

UNITY

A paragraph normally begins with a topic sentence stating the subject of the paragraph. All other sentences should build on the idea in that topic sentence. Do not bring in a new thought or irrelevant points that confuse the reader.

CONSISTENCY

Each sentence in the paragraph should be consistent in that it supports the main idea. Do not drag in contradictions of the main idea in the same paragraph. If there are contradictions, bring them up in other paragraphs.

ORDER

The sentences, ideas, examples, defenses, explanations, or detail supporting the main idea in the topic sentence should be in logical order. To illustrate, examples usually start by being broad and general. From there they move to being more specific.

STOP.

**THERE ARE SIX SENTENCES BELOW. PICK *THREE*
OF THEM AND COPY THEM INTO THE BLANK SPACE
IN THE FORM OF A GOOD PARAGRAPH.**

REMEMBER: The purpose of a paragraph is to take one
idea and expand it or defend it or explain it. A good
paragraph has unity, consistency, and order.

1. Athletes should not consume more than 30 percent of their calories as fat.
2. The body of a well-conditioned athlete conserves
   salt.
3. You should not do heavy exercise with food in
   your stomach.
4. Ideally, most fat should be unsaturated, that is,
   from vegetables.
5. Nuts are nutritious high-calorie sources of vegetable fat.
6. Sweets are no more desirable for athletes than for
   anyone else.

_____

_____

_____

_____

_____

_____

SUGGESTED SOLUTION

COMMENTS

THE PARAGRAPH

This is the only sentence that's logical. It has one central idea. The second sentence expands on the topic sentence. It makes a generalized statement that *expands* the main idea.
The third sentence moves from the general expansion to a specific example.

Athletes should not consume more than 30 percent of their calories as fat. Ideally, most fat should be unsaturated, that is, from vegetables. Nuts are nutritious high-caloried sources of vegetable fat.

THE RIGHT WORD

In writing, picking the *right word* is very important. That's because many words carry a variety of shadings of meaning. These can be the opposite of what you are trying to say if you don't know about those shadings and implications.

English teachers would tell you that each word has a DENOTATION and a CONNOTATION. What terrible technical words. I will put it more simply.

Words may often have two meanings:

DIRECT MEANING

This is the direct, specific meaning.

SUGGESTED MEANING

This is the association, flavor, implication, and aura of the word.

Several groups of words are listed below. Each word in each group has the same or close to the same DIRECT MEANING. However, they each have a distinctly different implied or SUGGESTED MEANING from all the other words in their same group.

TEACHER, PEDAGOGUE, MENTOR
•
WORK, TOIL, CAREER, DRUDGERY
•
BRAIN, EGGHEAD, INTELLECTUAL
•
INDIVIDUAL, NONCONFORMIST, NUT
•
WOMAN, LADY, FEMALE, CHICK
•
COP, OFFICER, FUZZ, CONSTABLE

The point is, of course, we must be careful to pick a word that makes clear the meaning we are trying to pass along.

FAST-TRACK REVIEW

Here is a fast-track review. COMPLETE THE BLANKS.

Some of the *negative* reasons people fear writing include:

Fear, Guilt, and _____

The Five Steps in getting an idea across are:

1. Idea in Your Brain
2. _____
3. Passing the Coded Message
4. Decoding the Idea Message
5. _____

The three filters that distort messages are:

1. Vague and Imprecise Meaning
2. _____
3. Trigger Words

The three myths of communication are:

1. _____
2. Big Words = Big Man
3. Safety Before Clarity

Name the ten rules of *A SUPER STAR* system of power writing:

A. Audience
S. _____
U. _____
P. Purge Pomposity
E. Everyday Language
R. _____
S. Stimulate the Reader's Interest
T. Tell Story Immediately
A. _____
R. Rest and Rewrite

A good sentence and a good paragraph focus on what?

_____

STOP.

WE NOW GO TO THE FINAL EXERCISE.

AT THIS POINT, OUR HOUR IS ALMOST UP. PLEASE GO BACK TO THE PARAGRAPH YOU WROTE AT THE VERY BEGINNING ON PAGE 10.

REVIEW THAT PARAGRAPH. APPLY THE TEN RULES OF *A SUPER STAR* SYSTEM OF POWER WRITING®. REWRITE WHAT YOU WROTE ONE HOUR AGO.

_____

_____

_____

_____

_____

_____

_____

_____

_____

YOU CAN NOW DO IT BETTER, CAN'T YOU?